TRAVELING SHOES

The Story of Willye White, US Olympian and Long Jump Champion

Alice Faye Duncan

Illustrated by **Keith Mallett**

CALKINS CREEK

AN IMPRINT OF ASTRA BOOKS FOR YOUNG READERS

New York

WELCOME TO GREENWOOD!
Home of hot tamales, kudzu vines, and cotton,
Mississippi mud, Delta blues, and
five-time Olympian—Willye B. White.

Willye laced her track shoes and ran around the world.
While money and fancy mansions would never be her fate,
Willye won shiny medals and broke world records.
Her fast feet blazed a trail for track legends and champions
like Carl Lewis, Jackie Joyner-Kersee, and Brittney Davon Reese.

No matter where Willye lived or traveled across the globe,
Mississippi was her motherland—the place that birthed
her vision, inspired her determination, and set her soul in flight.

With medals around her neck and luggage for the road,
the journey was not easy because life is filled with woe.
But if you follow Willye home or go back to the starting
block, lessons learned on the track point the way to victory.

Greenwood raised a champion—Willye B. White.

BABY NEW YEAR
(December 31, 1939)

I came into the world before the clock struck twelve.
It was almost New Year's Day in Money, Mississippi.

As Mama Willie marveled and gave me her first name,
Daddy Johnny sat in silence. He studied me like a book.

Johnny White did not beam or coo with bubbling joy.
There I was, his firstborn child, a boggling mystery.

I was an oddball baby with green eyes and reddish hair.
My body was a lump of dark blue veins and light-bright cocoa skin.

Mama Willie was pe-can brown and Johnny was midnight black.
Anger filled my daddy's face. He yelled, "This is NOT my child."

Mama Willie disagreed. But, her body was exhausted.
There was no energy to debate. Time would reveal the truth.

Johnny White was my father.
I was his strange magnolia.

But there on New Year's Day, he stomped and stormed
from the cropper shack and vanished in the morning mist.

When I was a baby, only three days old,
Mama Willie packed her bags and left me with her daddy.

Both of my parents ran away.
Rejection cuts like stone.

Forgiveness mends a broken heart.
Grace is the road to joy.

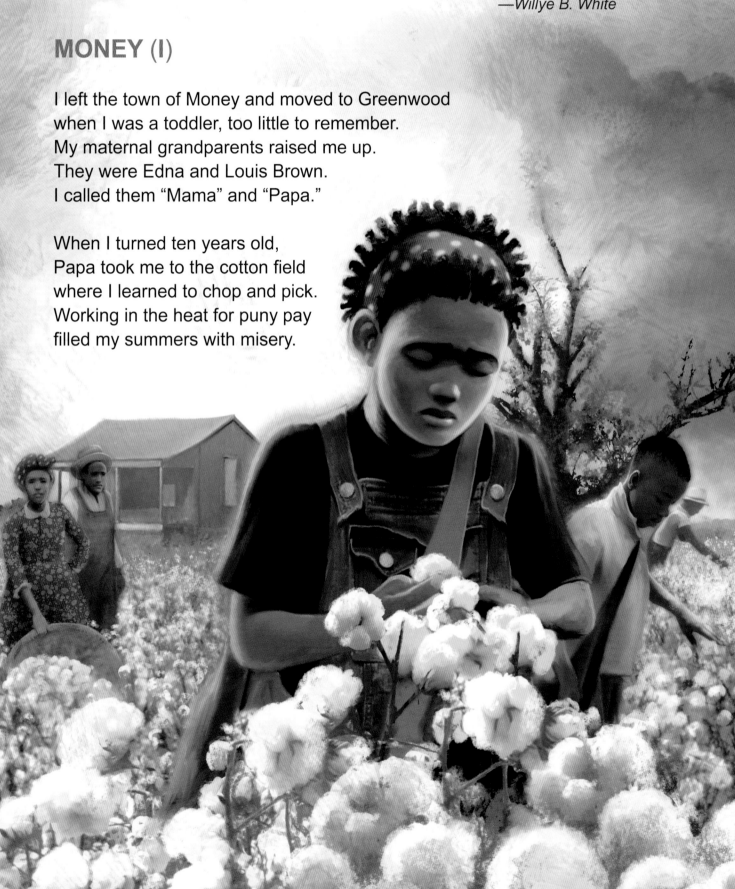

"My grandfather . . . insisted that I work in the cotton fields when school was out. . . . I worked there from sunup to sundown for two dollars a day. I hated it."

—*Willye B. White*

MONEY (I)

I left the town of Money and moved to Greenwood
when I was a toddler, too little to remember.
My maternal grandparents raised me up.
They were Edna and Louis Brown.
I called them "Mama" and "Papa."

When I turned ten years old,
Papa took me to the cotton field
where I learned to chop and pick.
Working in the heat for puny pay
filled my summers with misery.

I was never the smartest kid in school.
But, I was a mighty thinker, making plans
and dreaming above the clouds.
I wanted to fly, sail on ships, or catch some
train to a shining, thrilling place.

Old King Cotton was not my king.
What would be my golden ticket?

> "I was an outcast. . . . I had this funky red hair, and I was always running around in overalls with a dirty face and no shoes."
>
> —*Willye B. White*

WILD CHILD

Dressed in raggedy overalls with
itty-bitty braids all about my head,
I looked like Medusa from the ancient stories.

And when there was no cotton or chores to do,
like Atalanta in the age-old myth with her quick feet,
I removed my high-top brogan boots to rip and race,
up and down the dusty Greenwood streets.

I loved to run, jump, and dance.
I loved to laugh and sometimes I cussed.
I was Willye B. White . . . wild and free.
Many days I ran alone.

My loneliness was filled with friends
when Cousin Vee witnessed my fleeting feet.
She said, "I'm going . . . to try out for the track team."
Then she pleaded, "Why don't you come?"

I served my cousin a puzzled look.
She was a teenage kid in high school.
I was ten years old and in fifth grade.
Could I run track for the high school team?

Mama Edna gave me permission to follow Vee.
And since there was no regulation in 1950,
I tried out for track at the segregated school
called Broad Street High.

I was tiny, tough, and full of "big talk."
Confidence was my superpower.

Race one.
Race two.
Race three.
Race four.

NOBODY beat me.
I made the team.

"I was twelve years old when my mother died."
—*Willye B. White*

JOY AND PAIN

Grade-school girl with wings,
I played high school basketball.
Clouds blocked the sunlight.

My real mama died.
We shared no sweet memories.
Rain makes flowers grow.

> "Right over there is where Emmett Till was lynched.
> You remember Emmett Till, in the '50s?"
>
> —*Willye B. White*

MONEY (II)

I left Money, Mississippi, when I was a baby.
Papa moved us ten miles away for better employment.
He was the trusty gardener at the Greenwood library.

Like any town in the segregated South,
Blacks and whites lived separately and
no Black schools were funded equally.

I struggled to read in those days
because Mama and Papa could not help.
They were God-fearing, untutored folk,
my refuge, roots . . . two pillars of rock.

Homelife supplied the basic needs,
but death and danger surrounded me.
My real daddy died in 1955.
In that same year, when he was fourteen,
Emmett Till was lynched not far from Money.

Emmett's murder toppled America like a domino.
His mother's tears watered a seed in Rosa Parks.
When Mrs. Parks sparked the Montgomery boycott,
Reverend Martin Luther King Jr. caught the Holy Ghost.
His voice ignited the Civil Rights Movement.
People took to the streets waving protest signs.

My high school years were consumed with track.
I broke state records in the 60-yard dash.
As the fastest girl in the land of Mississippi,
my mind was made . . . the dream was set.

Dr. King would march to break Jim Crow's grip.
My integration plan was a different kind.
Willye B. would run to the mountaintop.

"[People] said, 'Oh, Willye, you can't make the Olympic team.' . . . They didn't know that I had a mission. And my mission was that I didn't want to go back to the cotton fields."   —*Willye B. White*

ED TEMPLE

Ed Temple coached women's track at Tennessee State University (TSU).
During the summer of 1956, he invited me to train on the Nashville campus.

Temple's famous track team was called the "Tennessee State Tigerbelles."
Edna and Louis shipped me off on a Greyhound bus. King Cotton had to cut me loose.
My dream was taking shape. I trained with college athletes when I was sweet sixteen.
Practice was required three times a day. It was rough and more rigorous than cotton.
Let the record show. My life flipped like a coin when I trained with the Tigerbelles.
Ed Temple drove us to the Olympic trials and I made my first US team in 1956.

"Australia was quite an experience. I discovered that there were two worlds. There was Mississippi and the other world. [In] the world outside of Mississippi, blacks and whites socialized together."

—Willye B. White

MELBOURNE SUMMER OLYMPICS (1956)

I trained for three months.
My event was the long jump.
It was a long shot.
The long jump was new to me.
I mimicked my opponents.

You begin to run,
accelerate, and take off
like a bird in flight.
I rode the wind in Melbourne
and won the silver medal.

I made history.
The books seldom mention me.
I am a footnote—
first American woman
to medal in the long jump.

First American
to set a dazzling record
and jump at the sun
farther than 21 feet,
like the flight of Icarus.

"[Ed Temple] taught me not to let one man determine your destiny."

—*Willye B. White*

SKEETER AND RED

When I graduated high school in 1959,
Tennessee State awarded me a track scholarship.

Ed Temple became my college coach.
He was a man with many rules.

I was an independent adventurer
on his team of Tigerbelles.

Like me,
Wilma Rudolph was a Tigerbelle
and teenage Olympian.

Friends called her "Skeeter."
Teammates called me "Red."

Formed from dust of the Jim Crow South,
we were female, poor, and Black,
sprinters, swift, and proud.

I was tiny and hot-tempered.
Skeeter was a poised gazelle.

And when Coach Temple's rules did not suit me,
I left for Chicago on a train in the winter of 1960.

Snow was my new archenemy.
Skyscrapers pierced the clouds.

Mayor Daley added my name to the city track club.
Willye B. White—undisputed long jump champion!
Chicago received me gladly.

"I trained from five to seven thirty in the morning, came home, got dressed, went to work, and at lunchtime lifted weights. . . . Then I'd go practice at three o'clock, and I'd run until seven. . . . I did that for twelve months of the year."
—*Willye B. White*

ROME SUMMER OLYMPICS (1960)

I earned a spot on
my second Olympic team
and worked as a nurse.
There was no rest from training.
Supreme skills made me heady.

I was built for speed.
Skeeter earned three gold medals.
The world praised her name.
Arrogance made me stumble
and Rome offered me no prize.

> "I came to the realization that athletics were my freedom. Freedom from ignorance, freedom from segregation. My athletics were my flight to freedom."
>
> —*Willye B. White*

LOUDER THAN A BOMB

It was 1963.
Children in Birmingham, Alabama, flooded the streets.
They filled the city jail in the name of justice and equal rights.
Little children made demands. They prepared for Jim Crow's death.
Nonviolent protests covered the South in a dizzy tear gas haze.

It was 1963.
Chicago children gathered near the track to watch me practice.
My beat-up track shoes pointed them toward a bright future.
The children mirrored my moves, my swagger, and stride.
Wrapped ankles preached my message louder than a bomb.

Champions prepare to win.
Hard work makes dreams come true.
Keep your luggage packed.

It was 1963.
I jetted off to São Paulo, Brazil, for the Pan American Games.
Overconfidence is a stumbling block. Self-assurance wins.
My mind visualized victory before my landing in a spray of sand.
I ran toward the board, raised my arms, and flew like an eagle.

It was 1963.
I took home the gold.

EQUAL RIGHTS NOW!
CIVIL RIGHTS ARE HUMAN RIGHTS
WE SHALL
EQUAL
END RACISM!
ALL MEN ARE CREATED EQUAL

"A family is not a mother and father and child;
a family is a group of people working for the same
common cause."
—*Willye B. White*

EVERY GOODBYE AIN'T GONE

When President Johnson signed the Civil Rights Act of 1964,
the Jim Crow signs came down and, during that October,
I traveled to Tokyo for my third Olympic Games.

Ed Temple was the US women's coach.
He never expected we would meet again.
However, life is an unpredictable journey.

And after Tokyo rains ruined my long jump,
Coach added me to the 4x100-meter relay team with
Wyomia Tyus, Edith McGuire, and Marilyn White.

We won the silver medal.
What is the lesson in this poem?
Teamwork is a priceless prize and
"Every goodbye ain't gone."

"I love life. People are always trying to take away my smile, but it's mine and they can't have it."

—Willye B. White

MEXICO MASSACRE

Listen, baby!
Life is sweet and sour like a chamoyada.
It was 1968.

Hoping to be heard,
teenagers spoke a desperate language.
Some threw bricks and broke glass.
They started bloody riots in America
when Dr. King was killed in Memphis.

As the contagion of unrest spread across the border,
I laced my shoes on a track in Mexico City.
A bummed leg hindered my long jump.
It was my fourth Olympic Games.

Outside the Olympic Village,
before the Games began
Mexican college students denounced
blind submission to authority.
Young activists demanded
fair labor rights.

National armed forces pretended to be deaf.
And hundreds of students died during the
Tlatelolco Massacre.

In solidarity with the Mexican students,
Tommie Smith and John Carlos
raised their fists on the Olympic podium

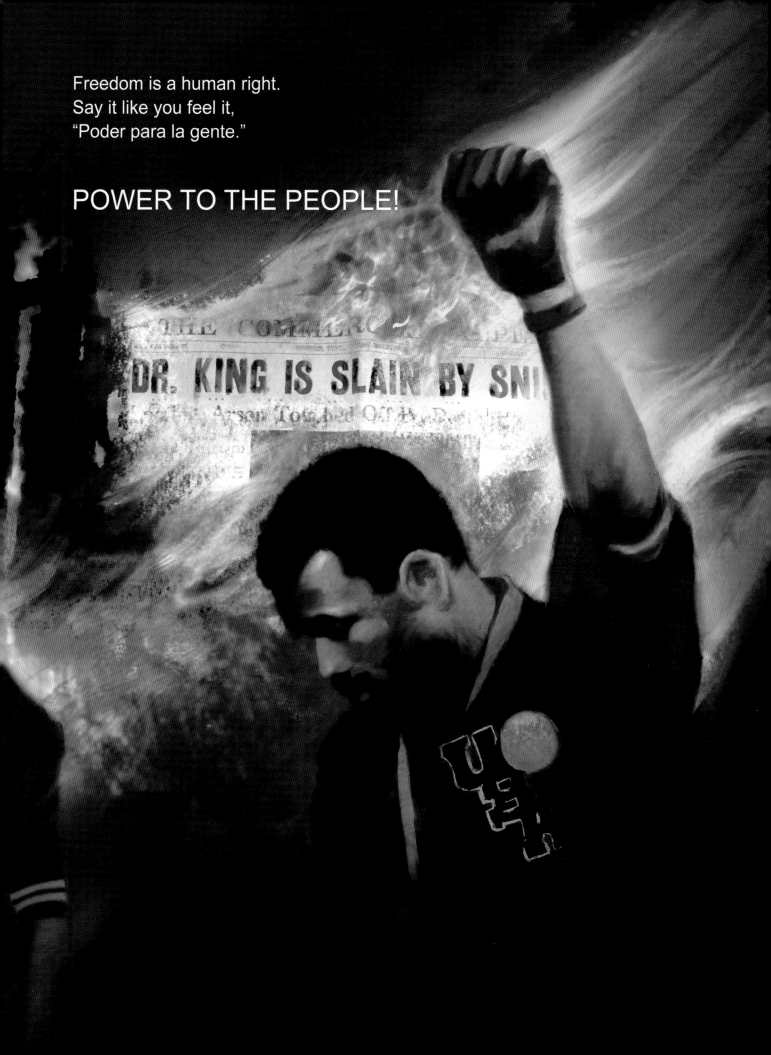

Freedom is a human right.
Say it like you feel it,
"Poder para la gente."

POWER TO THE PEOPLE!

"[After my first Olympic Games] I decided that I was going to travel all over the world, and that's what I did for the next twenty years."

—*Willye B. White*

MUNICH SUMMER OLYMPICS (1972)

Germany at daybreak
Terrorists waged acts of war
No medal
My fifth and final Games
Aching sorrow and well of tears
Big smile for the cameras

HALLS OF FAME

The halls of fame include my name.
Worn track shoes tell the story.
When you succeed and give your all,
people will still forget.

The halls of fame include my name.
Remember my joy and shine.
Winning is not effortless.
Practice is required.

The halls of fame include my name.
Sometimes you stand alone.
The starting block to grand success
begins with some great failure.

Greenwood raised a champion.
View the Olympic flame.
Before you win and take the prize,
winners must believe, "I CAN!"

"I believe in me."
—Willye B. White

The Making of Willye B. White

"I knew what was best for [me]. That is one reason why I turned from sprinting to the long jump. It is very technical. It requires thinking, strategy, not just power."
—*Willye B. White*

Willye White was the first American athlete to compete at five Olympic Games in track and field. White sprinted and jumped as a member of thirty-nine US international teams, including the first one to visit the Soviet Union in 1958 and the first to visit China in 1975. She won nine consecutive US outdoor championships and set seven world records. For nearly two decades, Willye was the best female long jumper in the nation with a career high of 21 feet, 6 inches.

Born in Money, Mississippi, White never lived with her parents, who died during her teenage years. Her maternal grandparents, Louis and Edna Brown, uneducated laborers, raised White in Greenwood. They considered education the cure to poverty. And despite her reading challenges, Willye White graduated from high school in 1959 and earned a college degree in 1976.

When she was ten, a cousin, invited White to try out for the Broad Street High School track team. Track changed her life. A gifted sprinter, running shaped her self-confidence. She said, "Athletics were my freedom. Freedom from ignorance, freedom from segregation."

While Olympic athletes trained without pay or corporate sponsorship in her day, Willye White devoted her body and soul to running because track offered her a free ticket to see the world.

At age sixteen, she participated in her first Olympic Games and won a silver medal in the women's long jump. Willye White was the first American woman to medal in this event. As a teenager, White went to school in Greenwood, but she trained during summers in Nashville, Tennessee, with Ed Temple. Temple was the women's track coach at Tennessee State University (formally known as Tennessee Agricultural & Industrial State College), a Historically Black College and University (HBCU). Training in Nashville was White's escape from the toil of picking cotton for two dollars per day.

Upon high school graduation in 1959, White joined Ed Temple's TSU Tigerbelles as a college freshman. Olympic gold medalists Wilma Rudolph, Wyomia Tyus, and Edith McGuire were part of this legendary team. Coach Temple nicknamed Willye White, "Mississippi Red." When Red began to socialize off campus and miss the team curfew, Temple cancelled her work-study scholarship. White withdrew from TSU in 1960 to work at a Chicago hospital and train for the Olympics with the Mayor Daley Youth Foundation.

Ed Temple met Willye White again in 1960 and 1964, when he coached the US Women's Olympic track teams in Rome and Tokyo. Coach Temple and White mended their differences. And during the 1964 Games, he added her to the 4x100-meter relay race. With Wyomia Tyus, Edith McGuire, and Marilyn White, Willye White won her second silver medal for the USA.

During her twenty-year athletic career, White competed in five Olympic Games from 1956 to 1972. She traveled to one hundred and fifty countries. It should also be noted that with unshakeable determination, Willye White established her whirlwind track career during the turbulent and transformative years of the American Civil Rights Movement. While Dr. King organized and marched in peaceful protests, Willye White contributed to Black progress with muscle and grit.

As she circled the globe, White won bronze, silver, and gold medals. At the end of her athletic career in 1972, she worked as a public health administrator who volunteered her time coaching student athletes and serving as a mentor and motivational speaker to Chicago youth. The indelible rhyme that she shared with children is the message that she lived. With a smile bright as sunlight, White would say, "If it is to be, it is up to me, because I believe in me."

Willye B. White died in 2007 from pancreatic cancer. To recognize her contributions to track and field, the City of Chicago named a park and athletic complex in her honor in 2008. You can visit Willye B. White Park at 1610 W. Howard Street, Chicago, Illinois.

Members of the 1960 Tigerbelles track team of Tennessee State University. Pictured from left to right are Mae Faggs, Wilma Rudolph, Lucinda Williams, Margaret Matthews, Isabelle Daniels, Willye B. White, and Coach Ed Temple. Temple called them the "Fabulous Six."

Timeline

1939 Willye is born to Johnny and Willie White in Money, Mississippi, on December 31.

1940 She moves ten miles south with her maternal grandparents, Louis and Edna Brown, to the town of Greenwood. They care for her until she graduates from high school.

1950 White joins the Broad Street High School track team when she is ten years old.

1952 Her biological mother dies. Willye White suits up for the varsity basketball team.

1954 The US Supreme Court ends racial segregation in public schools with a ruling in the case, *Brown v. Board of Education.*

1955 Emmett Till is lynched near Money, Mississippi. His death inspires the American Civil Rights Movement. Willye White's biological father, John White, dies.

1955 Dr. Martin Luther King Jr. helps to organize the Montgomery bus boycott to integrate city transportation in the American South.

1956 Willye White travels to Nashville, Tennessee, for the summer. She trains with Coach Ed Temple at Tennessee State University (TSU). She also qualifies for the Olympic women's track team in the long jump.

1956 She wins a silver medal in Melbourne, Australia. She is the first American woman to win a medal in the long jump.

1956 The Montgomery bus boycott is a success. City buses are integrated.

1957 The Greenwood newspaper calls White "a one-girl track team" because, as a high school sprinter and long jumper, many times she earned more points than entire teams.

1959 Willye White graduates from high school and enrolls at TSU to join the women's track team. She withdraws from college after the first semester.

1960 She trains with the Mayor Daley Youth Foundation in Chicago, Illinois. And she qualifies for her second Olympic Games in Rome, Italy.

1963 Black children in Birmingham, Alabama, form a children's crusade to rally against segregation. When they are jailed, President John F. Kennedy is inspired to support a federal law to abolish legal racial discrimination.

1963 Willye White earns her first gold medal in the long jump during the Pan American Games in São Paulo, Brazil.

1963 President Kennedy is assassinated in Dallas, Texas.

1964 Willye White qualifies for the Olympic Games in Tokyo, Japan. She wins a silver medal in the 4x100-meter relay event. It is her third Olympic Games.

1964 White breaks Wilma Rudolph's indoor 60-yard dash record of 6.8 seconds with a time of 6.7 seconds. President Johnson signs the Civil Rights Act of 1964.

1965 White starts work as a public health administrator in Chicago.

1965 She is the first American to receive the UNESCO Pierre de Coubertin World Fair Play Trophy for sportsmanship.

1967 She wins a bronze medal in Winnipeg, Manitoba, Canada, during the Pan American Games.

1968 Dr. King is assassinated in Memphis, Tennessee. Riots spread across the nation as people express their anger and dissatisfaction with racial inequality in America.

1968 White competes in her fourth Olympic Games. The host is Mexico City, Mexico, where students protest, demanding democracy, equality, and economic justice prior to the start of the Olympic Games.

1972 White competes in her fifth Olympic Games. The host city is Munich, Germany, where eight Palestinians invade the Olympic Village and kidnap several Israeli athletes.

1976 White trains for the Summer Olympic Games in Montreal, Quebec, Canada. However, she retires from sports due to injury and dedicates her life to coaching and public service.

1976 Receives her bachelor's degree in public health at Chicago State University.

1981 Willye White is inducted into the Mississippi Sports Hall of Fame and Museum.

1981 She is inducted into the National Track and Field Hall of Fame.

1988 She is inducted into the International Women's Sports Hall of Fame.

1999 White named one of the 100 Greatest Athletes in the 20th Century by *Sports Illustrated*.

2002 White named one of ten greatest female athletes by *Ebony Magazine*.

2007 Willye White passes away from pancreatic cancer.

2008 The city of Chicago names a park in honor of Willye B. White.

2009 She is inducted into the United States Olympic & Paralympic Museum Hall of Fame.

2018 Willye White is inducted into the National High School Track and Field Hall of Fame.

Author's Note

"Personality, baby. That is all I got."
—*Willye B. White*

It was the summer of 2015. While taking a drive through the Mississippi Delta, I passed a sign that welcomed me to Greenwood, "Home of 5-Time Olympian, Willye B. White."

I knew Lusia Harris, the Greenwood Olympian who scored the first points in the first Women's Olympic basketball game in 1976. But who was Willye B.?

What I learned when I googled Willye White's accomplishments was astounding. Energy to write her story did not arrive until 2021, when I remembered that Greenwood welcome sign.

During my research, I called a variety of athletes who were teammates and friends with White. Former Olympic swimmer and sportscaster, Donna de Varona, encouraged me to contact Pat Daniels Connolly. Connolly and Willye called themselves, "Soul Sisters." Pat Connolly is a retired pentathlete and college coach who trained US Olympians Evelyn Ashford and Allyson Felix. Conversations with de Varona and Connolly led me to contact former Olympians and TSU alumni, Ralph Boston and Margaret Matthews Wilburn. Each friend remembered "Red" as a resilient athlete with a charismatic personality. Their anecdotes offered me a three-dimensional view of Willye White's spunk, strength, and tenacity. She was a living example of independence, determination, and charm. May her life inspire readers to dream big, prepare to win, and keep their luggage packed.

Bibliography

All quotations used in the book can be found in the following sources marked with an asterisk (*).

Boston, Ralph. "I called her 'Tom Sawyer.'" Former university administrator and Olympian, Ralph Boston remembers meeting Willye B. White at a Mississippi track meet when she was fourteen years old. Phone interview with the author, Oct. 25, 2021.

Cheesebourough-Guice, Chandra. "Coach Ed Temple was tough but fair." Former Olympian and Tennessee State track coach remembers what it was like to train under Coach Ed Temple. Phone interview with the author, Oct. 26, 2021.

Connolly, Patricia Daniels. "We were soul sisters." Former pentathlete, Olympian, and track coach, Patricia Connolly remembers her 40-year friendship with Willye B. White, their shared Olympic Games under Coach Ed Temple, and their shared travels during and after their competitive athletic careers. Phone interview with the author, Oct. 15, 2021.

de Varona, Donna. "Running for her life." Former swimmer and Olympian, Donna de Varona, remembers meeting Willye B. White in Rome, Italy, at the 1960 Olympics. Phone interview with the author, Oct. 14, 2021.

*Dyer, Anna Presley. "Willye B. White" Digital Scholarship@Tennessee State University. digitalscholarship.tnstate.edu/cgi/viewcontent.cgi?article=1009&context=tsu-olympians.

*Harrell, Lorraine. "Willye White," *Chicago Tribune*, Mar. 10, 1991.

*Jordan, Pat. "From the land of cotton." *Sports Illustrated*, Dec. 8, 1975.

*LeBlanc, Diane and Allys Swanson. *Playing for Equality*. McFarland & Company, Inc., 2016.

*Lewis, Dwight and Susan Thomas. *A Will to Win*. Nashville, TN, Cumberland Press, 1983.

Lipsyte, Robert. "A Practical Woman with Dreams Intact." *New York Times*, Oct. 3, 1993.

Mitchell, Fred. "Celebrating the Life of a Pioneer—A gathering honors the late Willye White, who made an impact in athletics and beyond." *Chicago Tribune*, Feb. 11, 2007.

"Negro Olympic Star Paces Meet," *Greenwood Commonwealth* [MS], May 1, 1957, afternoon edition.

Park, Louis Hillary. "Willye B. White among state's hall of fame inductees." *Greenwood Commonwealth* [MS], Mar. 31, 1982.

Reed, Billy. "White extols Games—Five-Time Olympian saw new world in '56." *Courier-Journal* [Louisville, KY], Feb. 9, 1980.

*White, Willye B. Interview by Larry Crowe. The HistoryMakers Digital Archive. Session 1, tape 1, story 2, A2002.112, July 2, 2002. White lists her favorites.

*—— (The HistoryMakers A2002.112), interviewed by Larry Crowe, July 2, 2002, The HistoryMakers Digital Archive. Session 1, tape 1, story 4, Willye White describes her grandfather.

*—— (The HistoryMakers A2002.112), interviewed by Larry Crowe, July 2, 2002, The HistoryMakers Digital Archive. Session 1, tape 1, story 10, Willye White recounts her school years and early athletics.

*—— (The HistoryMakers A2002.112), interviewed by Larry Crowe, July 2, 2002, The HistoryMakers Digital Archive. Session 1, tape 2, story 1, Willye White remembers how she got into athletics.

*—— (The HistoryMakers A2002.112), interviewed by Larry Crowe, July 2, 2002, The HistoryMakers Digital Archive. Session 1, tape 4, story 9, Willye White discusses the rewards of her accomplishment for herself and her family.

Wilburn, Margaret Matthews. "Red loved to dance." Former Olympian and Tigerbelle, Margaret Matthews Wilburn, remembers what it was like traveling and practicing with Willye B. White during the 1956 Olympic Games in Melbourne, Australia. Phone interview with the author, Oct. 23, 2021.

"Willye White." *Olympedia*, olympedia.org/athletes/78009.

For Coach Billee Patricia Connolly —*AFD*
To Nia and Chris —*KM*

Acknowledgments

While researching blues music and historical figures from the Mississippi Delta, I discovered the inspiring life of Willye B. White. I owe the living texture of this text to a host of Olympic athletes who called Willye B. their sister and friend. They spoke with me to remember how "Red" gave them hope with her example of athleticism, love, and wit. Special acknowledgments go to Olympian and coach Billee Patricia Connolly. Like any good coach or editor, Billee Pat required me to rewrite and edit until my draft reached a winning form. Her contribution to my creative process was GOLDEN. Billee Pat! Thank you. Always.

Picture Credit

Tennessee State University: 35.

Calkins Creek
An imprint of Astra Books for Young Readers,
a division of Astra Publishing House
astrapublishinghouse.com
Printed in China

ISBN: 978-1-63592-580-7 (hc)
ISBN: 978-1-63592-581-4 (eBook)
Library of Congress Control Number: 2022951326

First edition
10 9 8 7 6 5 4 3 2 1

Design by Barbara Grzeslo
The text is set in Arial regular.
The titles are set in Arial bold.
The illustrations are painted digitally.